The Next Loves

The Next Loves

by Stéphane Bouquet

translated by Lindsay Turner

Nightboat Books
New York

Published originally as *Les Amours suivants*
by Editions Champ Vallon in 2013

Poems from this book have appeared in *Lana Turner Journal*,
Oversound, *Crazyhorse*, and *The Wolf*. The translator thanks the editors
of these publications.

ISBN: 978-1-64362-005-3

Cover image: Hervé Guibert, "Le seul visage, Plazy," 1981
Courtesy of the Estate of Hervé Guibert, Paris,
and Callicoon Fine Arts, New York

Design and Typesetting by Brian Hochberger
Typeset in Caslon

Cataloging-in-publication data is available from the Library of Congress

Nightboat Books
New York
www.nightboat.org

Contents

Les Amours...7

Solitude Week 1...25

Light of the Fig...35

Solitude Week 16...47

Translating Paul Blackburn ...53

East Side Story...61

The Covers...73

Solitude Weeks Autumn/Winter...85

For a Few Minutes of Sunshine...91

The Loves That Stay...99

Les Amours

I

His look and it took maybe 3
hello / seconds
only   his head underneath the blue hoodie
he takes off
because the rain is stopping   look here's
the planner's confirmation and
someone's holding an imaginary map of the conversation we'll say
that and that
the streets will be all orderly
if I stay close inside
the zones he surveys
but it isn't easy
imagining that the table and the lamp and the evening
sound like his breathlessness when he uncovers me and cleans

II

In the metro I look up from reading and
oh   he's holding flowers they're not for me
and a pastry-box
it's not for me   one more time where a face is a dangerous
hopeful landing
i.e. tomorrow hasn't yet deserted us   the proof is, you're
there   beginner at the edge
of human acts and your fear of coming back
unsmiled at   it'll be ok   if not I could instead
overwhelm you with affection   invent
sofas made of light
put them meticulously at the back
of the entrance to interior apartments where I'm waiting
      stretched against
the tenderness of *dasein*, or any other feeling of warmth

III

I run into   he's an ex, sort of
you've got an eyelash there on   take it off   I mean, caress
        he's with his brother
and his grandmother is   god rest her soul
he makes the movement of wings taking off and then there is
in the street and the second the light blackbird of death   at night
for consolation I'm with someone I barely
want   his face like a construction site
broken with acne I turn off
the light in order to believe
it's some loyal animal
licking at me in the now and now done
        ok it's ok I'll let myself be convinced he's only twenty
comes from Alaska even better another country
        where we could add in the embrace

IV

Each time I kiss the dealer
then suddenly often interrupted
paged urgent he's got to go comes back
      and each time I have to wait I imagine
crowds of addicts, epidemics
fortunately he's back always
in a flash as if by magic as if iron filings
in our skins as if
we were a series of + / - lined up and we
begin again oh today it'd be the unconditional
immanence of planet earth   I who tongue
his sharpened neck   he who shows the condom
politely for the right of entering
that joy   interior of ivy moving loudly in a wind

V

Red t-shirt and husky voice
we do yoga together   much less strong
than I am but so much more beautiful
at the end in savasana when we're supposed to become
one of those vibrations in the air and the ritual bell
sets us
almost behind absence I can only
think like an animal to live oh oh
oh that long slim desire
stretched out 2 meters away if I
rolled over on him really would that from now on be the only
hope of slowing
because of the sweetness in your bones
the quickness of death against which I recite a rose
        is a rose is a rose is a rose

VI

"Leave the warbling birds of May," said
the notice   yes and also leave Gregory who's not even
maybe
sixteen years old yet, naked in the sonnet
I find him at the edge
of the sidewalk he's actually shaking from the cold
in the snow that's starting again, winter's secret compartments
      but he stays
he persists he waits because
      this is the future promised from childhood
in the cold in the name of February   and his eyes are
blue and his Converse red
and I'm humming the softest
the softest petals of the flimsy primrose
at the very beginning when he gently spreads
the snow's legs, makes me bloom inside

VII

His screen name   Blue Adonis
6"1' 21yo top eyes blue cataract of blondness
& in my stupid heart the pure curare of beauty
        Wikipedia says Adonis is a minor god
associated with herbs and the burning of incense
and according to Lucretius smell
is the secret nickname of all things   so here Blue Adonis
since the dawn of time I've been burning
fragrant hope so you'll agree to come / come
I'll pay for the taxi and more if you want
it's nothing it's almost
normal to spend crazy amounts
so that a minty-fresh mouth
forms once more the only divine command / come

VIII

Seeing as Pindar's become so much silence
& indecipherable stuff, someone
has to be consecrated to sing of the skier
with wings of the dawn and that ambitious fleece   "I came here
to win it"   the TV delighted to circulate his
post-adolescent smile   o champion   *o mégiste*
ton mégiston   o special golden
winter's falcon and next, imp in motion
over the ice   o panting
with the effort of the chase   o tight secret stretches
near the navel with hair as dense
as my desire and their hibernation
take refuge in your deep crevasses   o
cock of thick snow now gathered and received
so happily here   o Jason Lamy-Chappuis

IX

His name is Simon I think but
maybe he has another name in
rooms where someone catches
kisses and calls him Simon
we'll be trapped, displayed together
on a shelf made for peacefulness, Ikea variety, the type of wood
that's cheap and white   every morning he makes coffee
       he's in his underwear and or else
naked in the variations of light   there's nothing
besides the serial logic of days, one two
and the 363 the rest of the Euler sequence to live I know it's
scientifically pointless Simon it's crazy
how we still want can you pass the coffee please
you who rub your nose and scratch your stomach and finally
leave in bed the trembling odor of the morning

X

And then afterwards we left
together & by car he drives
the icy sun strikes villages painted blue-gray
    impossible to park anywhere safe
for four nights running we can't just
leave it / hop on the train he loves   the highway
is empty the GPS in charge of the way we talk about
the climate conference Cancun
yadda yadda it all sounds like his voice
and here's the unexpected story
    once upon a time 1 & 1
are given some time together the same air
carried within a little metal shell itself as fragile
and itself as easy to crush

XI

When after the event the champion caresses
very sweetly sorry the head of Eric Ress   what luck
for the atoms of air accidentally crushed
in the joy of the consoling touch   Pindar
perhaps we should democratically
sing of the opposite, sing of the glory of losers as well   o Eric
Ress French-
American swimmer scion of Indiana's campuses
8th and last   and the next day I too go swimming lap
after lap   down there I join his sweat
the disappointment in his bedroom self-accusations of
          weakness the poplars
out the window in extraordinary autumns
          indeed champion look at me
look at me also   more than likely to lose

XII

I remember perfectly
the pill of testosterone left sitting one day on the red couch
in the café where I'd go   the servers
would say hey you when I walked in   it's been years
I'm still sucking that endless
hormone candy   maybe he's checking me out in silence
making up excuses to bump into sketching out
the street map of the meeting, new life chapter 9
        inside I call him Laura
but plural my
Lauras my Beas my loves
the result was ever after
to count to 14
as the perfect number of times I would have touched you

XIII

In the film Casey
Affleck knocks out his girlfriends with his fists
& kills them   I'm sitting
next to Kenneth
but it's no good jumping on him he'll just
squirm out with a smile   in the film
we're told that a house is
peaceful if the chairs
are pulled up around the table &
the eggs are sizzling in the skillet & there's someone
we draw closer like trusting little rabbits
and he kills us and the house was quiet
and the world
was calm

XIV

On Facebook someone posted & thanks
a youthful face reading a poem
"Soonest Mended" it was called   we'll be
soonest mended if and only
if you come closer, saying the words   we are
all chatty
it's true but under the talk solutions lie everywhere
intertwined from the outset   I start you over on repeat
bright reader of the poem Adam Fitzgerald as
it were   everything is verifiable lasts
4 min 51 seconds   you're speaking   you're saying
         with and sometimes without
solitary and hopeless and still everything's
reassuring because of your scarf around your neck because
of the world from now on & from now on real

XIV'

(I'm not going to let you leave like that
on Youtube others have shared
their thoughts about you   UR A QT says heyyoumillionaires
     which is really
completely true   thanks says
dinnerbucket9 to
"the tireless molecules of
your scarf, to all the roaring
tribes inside it"   for him too then
you open the channels of the plural
     I'm going to translate
my Poem 14 and post it
respond if you want it's
no big deal above all what counts is just talking the proof
you see I've already added one more comment)

Solitude Week 1

day 1: a very simple poem about
being in the street about
seeing the people about wanting
them too to contribute

to the relocation of hope, closer to us

(night)

at the supermarket, in the aisles
buying 2 chocolate yogurts
are they equivalent to the waiter from yesterday
night, flying, Corsican restaurant

blond elf Peter Pan superhero
of service

so thin his skin lay
directly
on his bones the 2 yogurts

aren't the cheapest
ones, are they equivalent
to the light that falls sometimes

adding districts
to the brightness

day 2: the metro keeps running, imperturbably
it's like us

we can't ever
really not-want
still to belong
in the crowd of carts at the checkout

whole shelves full of produce
and in the neon aisles, I
calculate a possible price

where people come up to me and ask

day 3: or: the world
has happened

already and all that's left
    -have a coke and a burger
    -learn the names of all the Celtic tribes
    -get used to transparency
which is the 3rd or 4th secret death reveals

(evening)

self-portrait with carnivorous hip-thrust
24 / 7 / 365
reciting the mantra of sharing: try

to take part warmly
for once

don't let winter
get ahead

it's true for sure that there are
almost everywhere public
squares of death and markets
illegal markets where people sell themselves

    their poverty

but please: we could stop
wanting
we, starting with you

day 4: this is the type
of Econ 101 lecture I'm trying to give: the violent
inequalities of supply
and demand, or that all things besides
a face follow
the law of diminishing returns or that

in the non-commutative world

the sentence, I'm coming towards you
annuls, *de facto*, the ideal place where

sun gladiolus lakes in the parks where crows
can drink, & other kinds of birds
you're coming towards me

day 5: "casual Friday," we've all
worked a ton
even if the kids would say no

a *shit*ton, I'm thinking of
us finding each other this weekend I'm thinking of

something as beating-fragile
as a sliver / cut in the heart of a bird

(night)

another lesson on: money is
a tool for counting, store of value, pillar
of social order, and above all equivalent so general that
the equation
for a partially commutative world
is really very easy

I'm coming towards you
if we add $150 or $200
= now you're running to me

(night)

we spend the evening on the sofa and he says in no particular order
-I had a rough day
-I'm taking care of things
-I grew up on Facebook
-it's midnight when are you turning into

the big bad wolf I suppose
is always there in the first kisses too long
delayed

etc. and so to live
finally I did get some other sentences out of him
the trick now is to bury them
here, like certain animals do
to store up for hard times, for example him

who I've just sucked off again
then quick into Homeric deep-freeze
but then you were just a filthy cock
and from now on you're like
the gods who rule the vaulting skies

Light of the Fig

I imagine the crocuses also sometimes come down unexpectedly
     feverish, spreading
their long green leaves through the wrong season. So it's
     October 7. We're living
an Indian summer: hot and a little empty maybe but at least
     we're living. Lots of people
laugh in the street. The primary examples of existence
     include:
someone says hi like he wanted to sleep with you but knows
     simply and sadly
that he won't. Or it's your own wild translation from
     the wet fringes
of his voice to a word less and less likely:
     hope. Nevertheless
we're alive. Tyler Clementi, Seth Walsh, Asher Brown, and
     Billy Lucas
are dead, 18, 13, 13, 15. The only way to escape
     their enemies.
You, you were luckier in the end when
     you were 12
they chased you with their knives, they were such
     sensitive animals
they could smell what you didn't even know. But you,
     you had paws
strong enough to dig out your tunnels and get away
     and now
you place sad stones, so completely hardened
     with sadness
along the alley of the absences. You're there now in the dead
     space of their acts of love, you never
pray but once in a while you make promises:
     next time
I'll make myself a part of it, I'll be for & be thinking of you.
     Oh my god
in fact it's already happened and putting the condom on him
     I knew I was becoming you.
He was called Nurettin. Light of the fig, it means. It's so poetic
     immediately

a shower of gravelly violet light. We're sitting
        between two
purple rhododendron bushes on a cold stone bench
        "Probably 'bush'
and '*buisson*' have the same origin" "Probably" although really I
        have no idea.
The clouds seem like they want to pull a sheet of metal-gray
        at all costs across the sky,
maybe it's going to rain, the garden empties expectantly,
        but it didn't rain
and we played out one ridiculous game
        of seduction.
The pinky finger in his language is called hummingbird because
        of its twig-like fragility.
And another one finally later we ended up in my bed "I
        don't have much
experience" "No it doesn't matter, experience is about
        sexual pleasure
inexperience is about immortality," it came out like that in
        pseudo-English
because immortality needs a global language. The strangest moment
        is when he stops rimming me to rinse his mouth
with rubbing alcohol. But ok. Of course one of the poets I dream
        of being
already objected to displays like these. This poet would prefer
        that my own night
speak my lines: some fruits have shells that are fuzzy
        and plush
and there you'd be received—but it's useless with these dead
        almond trees. Or put another way:
"there is no empty time in people's lives" (Arlette Farge). This,
        for example,
is a morning: incandescent like all the mornings on which it's
        still possible
to get up and add some hours to the biography.
        Justin Aaberg,
Raymond Chase are dead. 15, 19. If it means anything, I willingly
        dedicate to you

the improbable temperatures of October 10. Oh look
    the next next day
rolling in for us, and with it childhood's child crouched against
    the morning light.
On his face: anxiety, anticipation. But surely it's
    not today
he's going to meet the big dark unknown
    promised
by certain horoscopes. Surely not today, or ever. You,
    just now,
so far from that child, you've got Nurettin. Each time you
    make love
you bury yourself frantically into his chest
    as if he
could keep you from sinking any deeper into goodbye. But
    as soon as he leaves
the backlash: what's left? Nothing, autumn, the leaves
    shrivel
dry and burning, then they flee into the void. Paid by the city,
    the gardeners
rake them pile them throw them into trucks
    and it's over.
Probably no one asks them, say, would you rather
    be incinerated
or serve as fertilizer in the next world? And if we're
    lucky enough to attend
the next showing of the young trees, the saddest part is that
    they'll be
other leaves and we'll have so few weeks to learn
    to recognize them
to know the name of each one. Speaking of names, in
    Beverly Hills 90210
Ian and Teddy's love affairs seem to be going well, that's
    just about how
we're living, isn't it? As far as possible from our disappointments,
    as close as possible
to the tally of days taking place, even if they're filled with
    trash tv.

Oh it's intoxicating the chase, the gull always in flight
        refusing
and refusing to come down and land on death.
        Actually
to be less specific: the chase is intoxicating period.
        Otherwise
October 15 is a day of dingy foam, the fall having
        thrown itself
into the cold currents with its head down. This morning however
        there's something
blinking a friendly message from Nurettin full of Turkishisms
        if that's
how you say it and it reminds me of the auto-translated
        email from Cuba:
"Already I want to have you in me some arms so that you do
        to me all that
you finish saying to me, have much need of you." It's
        undeniable
that their faces are all the more splendid, flickering
        as they can
in language, undeniable that all you do is add the right amount
        of sentimental sun.
After which you watch them appear. Like exactly
        3 weeks ago
at the foot of Poseidon's temple in white ruins at Sounion
        "the marble
from this region is less durable and corroded by the salt"
        said the guide
she wouldn't stop talking about the sea-god, I wanted
        to interrupt
no god is only the god of some one thing, brush up
        on your polytheism,
they all work together to ensure their survival, and
        ours with it
but wisely I kept listening and it wasn't
        completely useless either
problems with the gold mines and food supplies
        and the economy

and Attic navigation in the classical age right up until she says
    you have
40 minutes of free time. Immediately someone's sitting
    at the top of the cliff
someone who contained within him a young virgin priestess and
    who waited and who was hoping
in the end, 18 minutes left, that the silhouette of god would rise
    above the fishy sea
and it happened: from here, rocks and tawny earth, tourists
    and buses
both invisible and inaudible because of the wind, and the present
    emerged from the climate
& spread itself over things, which is to say that she and the one
    who contained her had
above all the impression that the world had struck them, gently,
    tenderly. Don't worry
it murmured I only want to say that we're alive.
    Cody Barker,
Zach Harrington are dead. 17, 19. You back then
    they made you lick
the tiled floor and beat you in the high school stairwells but
    it would've taken
a much more penetrating enemy to make you stop there with
    so little and so
quick. "How can I die, I who have never lived? I who have never
    roamed a moor to meet him!" (Balzac).
The strategy was to go down and breathe the communal and
    more rarely mortal sphere
of language beneath adolescent shelters of silence, to become
    the perfect pupil
of continuity, not brilliant but perfect and industrious. In fact
    if I could have
I would've taught you all: it's not hard to add sentences
    and days
without losing anything along the way. One day it rains.
    One day it's dry and cold.
Today there's rain and a face above lambswool reading
    in the café

and that on the other hand is a mortal danger: suddenly
    the songs on the radio
all seem to have the same secret refrain: everything's over or
    rather it's terribly
about to end. Before, I would have had
    some stirring things to say
because all the windows started shaking with
    the emotion
of his departure, but I don't have time for it now.
    Nurettin called to say
he's on the way home from school. Of course, one of the poets I
    dream of being wouldn't include
so much circumstance. The poet who would say that a smile
    alone will tell me
open my face to him and it will reveal, if I come down
    to live in constraint
where all the verbs have lost their singulars, the grand écriture
    understood by trees
and the society of animals. But the truth is that
    Nurettin had
"The Aging Population and the Retirement System"
    or something
like that and that he's only going to help me cross
    the bridge of hours
and leave me gently on the other side of anguish. Is that
    where I've
arrived? October 22. Colder and colder, so cold that
    no more flies
beat themselves stupidly against the windows, what a shame,
    I like
the flies and all the insects that aren't trapped by the desire
    to say *I*
within the species. Imagine a world without
    the first person where everything
started with *you*, with *them*. Bumblebee honeybee dragonfly
    short-lived cricket
look the countries arise and it's enough to flutter
    innocently

from one to the other. If I weren't so tired I could invent
    for us
an electric lavender for automatic honey, greenhouses
    for butterflies, thickets
teeming with caterpillars, a burgeoning anonymous happiness.
    But I don't even know
what time I went to bed last night. At Édouard Ropars's party
    there were
people I hadn't seen in forever—which means forever
    had time
to have passed—and also a beautiful bearded architect, that
    superfluous type of shepherd boy
and I thought, I could trust him with the construction
    of my tomb
and later: in such alleys of the species someone has died it's not
    very
important but it's not negligible either. Such coincidence this
    morning,
another surge of morning, another darling timid morning,
    I find
in my inbox the photo of a soldier who's sweeping
    the alleys
of a military cemetery after a volcanic eruption. A friend
    has remembered
that more than anything I like putting the days in order, endlessly
    counting out the rhythm of things,
which is to say everything that needs to be evacuated immediately
    from death also I love
to sweep just to keep the territories of the fare-thee-well a little
    in the light. Poets
without borders, that's the organization I'm in charge of,
    every day it issues
bulletins of survival. It's October 25 and we're alive.
    Brandon Bitner is dead.
14. There's nothing much to add: maybe the color
    of the sky, maybe
the group of pigeons flying in the color of the sky, maybe the
    stale brioche

I had at 9:42 this morning. 5:38 this evening I just re-read
    Coleridge's conversations
he talked to someone too, wanted to talk
    to someone
made up little characters in the form of pronouns and there
    you have it. "To thee, for whom
No sound is dissonant which tells of Life." There's still *indeed*
    so much gossip to share
even if there's no news of Ian and Teddy, almost like
    they've been
kicked off the show. The same show doubtless
    so interesting because
actors of 32 play high-schoolers of 17. Maybe out there in
    Beverly Hills
it's a micro-climate of eternal stagnation, maybe some bizarre
    fold in time
that superposes the ages. Their *modus vivendi*. On the other hand
    for us,
as someone was saying last night at dinner, it's as if
    it were raining
ceaselessly on stage and we dried ourselves off against each other.
    It's our *modus vivendi*.
In any case, it's a matter of carving some space in
    the moment
always emerging from new verbs. A strangely warm day
    happened
and when I re-read that last sentence I'm not quite sure
    I understand it
surely I wanted to say that I prefer verbs to nouns
    and now
probably sentences to verbs and even more the stubborn ivy
    that spreads
everywhere warmly wrapping the pillars and
    the windows
of the library where we read, filtered red autumn
    just at the moment
when the doors open. Oh beware fantasy.
    It'd be better to focus

on the documentaries of morning, when Nurettin turns
     over in bed
and lightning, his shoulders wide as seagull wings close back
     on the dawn
& me inside it. One of the poets you imitate mutely says that the
     broken torsos
of antique gods hide fortunes or predictions for the future, i.e.
     change your life.
But you think instead that Nurettin shelters
     all murmurs and all whisperings. This is a morning: astounding
by definition. It's October 31 and feels like spring
     again
except the leaves have already broken into the dry zone
     of the end. A fly
lets itself be fooled and is buzzing, poor thing, tomorrow she'll
     be dead again from cold,
exactly 17 years ago a young man named after a river lost
     his heart
at the exit of a club. 23. Overdose, heroin and cocaine.
     Not us.
We've lived up to now and now we're going to get through
     one more winter
even if a certain number of our species surely won't.

Solitude Week 16

Dear Your Highness who lives in me:

When you dawdle a long time musing
in the halls of the *schloss sanssouci*
out of pure love for the parquet floors

do you really think it's going to be enough
to close to open your eyes
so you can breathe anew the powdery glamour of the wigs

where you'll stop being lonely
and without favorites but for the moment

all your panicked servants
are rushing so fast to prepare your way

towards immense personal terraces where
only absence waits on you

it seems like even the trees there want to help

&

Before when you were
so little so breath so nothing

someone arranged your massy hair
on your bare shoulders & your child's tricks

time was only the condition
of the possibility of you

and nothing was ultimately expected
to overtake you in the winter

&

He was across the street

now you just want
to touch him, the interior landscape of his thighs

as soft you imagine as the most secret
goose-down or
the literal translation of a word without world

&

In the kitchen someone's calling you
to share

hunger & newspaper-ink of dawn, you smell
soap on sale
he says & laughs & to eat, the whole hope's invented of course

but it's better like this
for taking the slow pulse that's indispensible

to the solidity of the house
shining in the breath-lit lamps
where some consoler lets in

2 by 2
ok we, finally fragile

&

Sometimes you go out incognita
your real face ever more hidden
behind your age, nightmarish fan
all the boys who ran
they come kneel
docile things for the girls who come out
after you and you
only you cough
in your dress getting dustier

& you cry without any sadness
just out of actual allergy
to scattering death

Translating Paul Blackburn

solitude weeks 27 – 31

If without delay
you call (go on)
212-613-1717

                    a fabulous giant apartment

could still be yours

with a view over the river
& the summer twisting itself around mouths
& over the gas-fume haze

       which envelops, saturates, the ducks
       the little blue-haired lady
       drinking water out of the fountain

and the heat, egalitarian
also embracing
the banks' surprise profits
blinking on the southern horizon

       and those thighs, the boy's, beneath his bermuda shorts and
          the subdued thumping of the helicopter

plus the girl making a date with someone
she's almost positive it'll be great, come

       exaggerated persuasion and come
       that she repeats all, please really *oh*

please she must be thinking of
caresses that outline her shoulders

On the street you meet
       police & firefighters the neighborhood
       sirens turn the world a
       video-game euphoria

a guy who says to his friend
           still
you know and the gesture, *down,*
of his hand

in context maybe

           calme   •   *tranquille*

in the calmed and sleeping landscape you'd be simply
buried

                    in the goodness

                    of time (I just breathed
                    on the miniscule red spider
                    running across goodness)

someone like him would have come
in spite of his workplace schedule
just *still* & his

wake-up kiss

in the stretched-out afternoon

The white-haired black saxophonist who starts
playing at 7am   •   the morning   •
                                        is deserted

it's an effort of the night or maybe
special vestige
of the old legends when the city literally
sweated
with love

worn out sigh of we remember when
to have read it and better
the day goes on impervious like

the conveyor belt in the bagel toaster
the untranslatable square
            in the sun & July
the kids playing on a half-flooded
block of concrete and

            all
            that jazz
the Sikh talking with the girl the fountain
seal   also worth it

even though I accept the children:
their more efficient p r e s e n t participles
i.e. the ones you hear in living
                        yelling
                              following

Including the photographer his bare
flat perfect stomach that required
hours and years of work he strolls towards
               the end
of the pier for his stupid photo of an excessive sun

falling
straight in between two buildings
at the same time it's plainly impressive

nuclear explosion in reverse
as if the light swallowed itself
in its stomach of light
                    if that makes any sense at all

but no more intense than
          / on further consideration /
          the orange nova of the evening sun
          tucking itself bird-like into the green trees

          we head towards Park Slope to dine
          at the best Italian restaurant
          in Brooklyn, supposedly

and it was vaguely true and very long and now
the trees and the night
the scavenging rat remain
          & Habib repeats: it was good

Finally I gave up
            overwhelmed
counting the powerful ankles
in this city, even the ones behind which
I'm walking *right now*

ultra-blond   •   super-rivery

if only he knew: it would take so little
to be saved but ok

I just go straight to dinner—
the building bizarrely lost
in an instant of nowhere
between the R
            and nothing

night falls the wind
picks up the storm   we close the windows
tip out buckets of second-light

we eat blueberries we listen
to the voices of Paul and Frank

and why have I
suddenly a mouthful of tears

for not having known

how to protect them? from death no matter if I wasn't really
born yet of course
            (remember the
            falling rain)
I could have made the effort

East Side Story

On the last day we climb the hundreds of thousands of steps up
    to the top
of Elephant Mountain, it's the city's ritual excursion because of
    the general need
for fresh air, because of the subliminal slogans: you too,
    get active!
So many families you could say the hillsides
    are crawling
with children, a five-year-old boy concentrating
    hard, heave ho,
holding his face up at each step towards applauding parents,
    what a shame
we can't hang him like a protective medallion
    around our necks.
Step number 2300, by now it's just us among the vegetation,
    gingkos and
other unspecified trees and that, *watch out,* he says,
    local species
of gluttonous mosquito, among the endless droning
    Buddhist prayers
in the temples, the traffic shrinking farther and farther away
    down there. And
by chance a shelter, boards, blue tubs, lost tires,
    a little hut
in a dirty clearing overlooking the immenseness
    of the city. Sitting
together we confirm the course of things, time passes,
    apparently in Japan
the medieval Buddhist poets would say love = dim your light
    in order to mingle
with the dust, maybe it's true. Then when
    night falls
I fight back tears deep at the back
    of a fried-chicken place because
mango and so beautiful, the yellow flesh unsheltered from its
    skin is the face
of his last gift, our 4 hands clenched beneath the table, *don't go*
    he says *I don't*

know what to say and then some others come sit down next to us
       gratuitously ruining
the adieu *I'm not sad 'cause you're not going are you?* he says
       and then at the end
of course we're done in by the orders of separation. The kiss takes
       completely off
by motorbike from here out between the two pillars, Jianguo
       North Road section 1.

And the day before the last day,
I'm particularly exhausted, 5 days straight of 20 hours awake, he
       delicately *ssh!*
takes off me everything that might keep me from sleeping, shirt
       pants socks
but not underwear, which on the contrary will stop
       the drifting towards. I know that
all of this is almost over, he too wears the sad smile of the
       almost-empty
room and the soon-to-be-renounced caress, he says, if you never
       take any pictures
is it because you think words are better souvenirs?
       No doubt but I was
wrong today, you've got nothing but a pronoun for a face.
       I forgot
what night it was but I remember the dark blue elevator
       where I ask why
the hotel doesn't have a 4th floor. Because *chi* means 4 and city
       and poem
and death depending on the different tones. *According to you*
       he says (I translate it now), does
language have meaning or is it completely arbitrary?
       According to me what counts
is to keep talking, language must have meaning if
       we can reduce it
to equations like poem = city + death = 4 but talking is
       the only way
of orienting ourselves in the manufacture of hypotheses
       where a later world

is possible. It is possible to climb the hill together tomorrow
     like the little god
of endurance and find an obliging clearing and maybe a bench
     and a stupendous view out
over the traffic that we needed to share. *Seriously?*
     he says,
voice and look incredulous. When he has exhausted
     his sweetness undressing me,
he sits at the foot of the bed watching cartoons with the volume
     low and in spite of everything I fall asleep.

2 days before the end we go
for an hour by motorbike, it's 1 in the morning, I cling
     to his stomach, I've slid my hands
beneath his jacket and his t-shirt to caress his breath and not
     to fall, bends and hills, where are we
going, surprise, *be not afraid*, the breeze a little cold
     despite
the reassurance of his back. We're in hot yellow baths
     of sulfur.
The employee gestures with an indifferent finger towards
     the private rooms, cabin 13, floor
flooded, we're naked and our things on the shelves, the water
     seems to spout directly
from the tap of the goddesses of immortality. He laughs, he says,
     what if we kiss
hard behind the steam rising over these old wash drawings,
     he teaches me how to distinguish
the *song* movement of his tongue in my mouth,
     the *tang* movement
of his tongue in my mouth, his teeth dangerously grazing
     the poetry of the western renaissance:
mouth full of ivory gravel, tiny little things hidden beneath
     the cushion
of his lips, it's 4 in the morning, I yawn and I have to work
     tomorrow but must stay
longer to survive longer, even more years, each kiss
     profoundly

thought out in the very few days of the two of us.
　　　Also the fog had fallen
on the hills on the way back, the rain, also, falling on the bike.
　　　He wants me to drive so that
he can take his turn sleeping on my back, can also rest
　　　in the zone of provisional
certainty but the road is wet, the fog encircles us,
　　　I've never
driven a motorbike, I don't want everything to end up in death
　　　already. He says
I don't really believe, at his age, in death. But me, I do, in fact
　　　enough for the two of us.

3 days before the end, another very late night,
after his part-time job. He motions towards the other half
　　　of his chair
for me to sit close to him, *wo* and *ni* are the first Chinese words
　　　he teaches me, and it's
legitimately logical (me & you) given the neighboring dialects of
　　　our faces. Slowly I copy
the ideogram but mess up, he re-does it stroke by stroke:
　　　we start
with the radical 我 and then we add the flourishes, 我
　　　is pronounced ge, means axe
or halberd, instantly I hear the interminable sadness
　　　which floats sometimes
to the surface of language. If I = axe, do I believe that
　　　from the beginning
we're violently separated and how to be 100% sure that language
　　　is sometimes
wrong, that speaking's enough to invent a shelter
　　　for our arrival, and
if in Chinese *we* is *wo men* / literally, me several,
　　　do you think
a collective word could ever be guaranteed? But I don't say
　　　anything to him
about the burning swells of solitude, like when you have to take
　　　a Pepcid

because the esophagus has filled with acid rain or acid fear.
   He only wants
to know the right way to pronounce the word
      Sarkozy, the cars go by
without stopping on the downtown highway out the windows of
      the hotel.

4 days before the end, we're walking towards
Daan Park at an hour sunk deep into the night,
      the too-tropical autumn
of global warming, because—not that he's told me but—
      maybe
there's an ice-cream place still open and he wants a scoop
      of mango. In fact
it's closed, rats and stray dogs running through the park,
      I'm not supposed
to kiss him because of the surveillance cameras, you're in Taipei
      you know and besides
he says (I'm translating), don't be too good to me or
      I'm going to miss
even the inside of your mouth which I taught him could be
      caressed, even
the back caverns protected from the teeth by the soft slug
      of the tongue.
That night, in the park's alleys, deserted except for
      some kids singing
in a kiosk and us, sitting on the concrete risers
      in the amphitheater,
I make up one surname for him, since I don't know how
      to pronounce Yi Jui, and he prefers
not to teach me, as if it'd be better for me not to be able
      to call him anything
and for us to live anonymously, or as if he wanted to be
      that type of god you can't even pray to and thus
I baptize him the symbol which suits him best. For hurry up
      for example I say
common sense go go go because this has become almost the landscape
      of the common solution.

Apparently in medieval France, lawyers would say
    love = use and
profit of the common land where everything's endless,
    inexhaustible.

5 days before the end,
the first day we roamed the streets by motorbike, I'm totally lost
    he takes care
of everything, ordering black tofu sticky rice balls
    stuffed with sesame
red bean soup, mixing sugar into the pallid yellow grains
    & pouring
boiling water over it, it's just a night market,
    he smiles
like the consequence of a Chinese poem
    where the transparent fog
melts the banks of old snow and you can't tell anymore
    if the whiteness is
snowflakes or plum-blossom petals or crane-eggs, but anyway
    a voice
is spreading on the wind from the orange tree and the songbirds
    come back again once more from winter to celebrate
the real moon, the awakening, the *bunda* of things.
    The next market, it's 1 in the morning,
it's overflowing with people buying and wearing a ton
    of useless things, moon boots
scarves hats, because that's how winter is defined
    in other countries
and it's less terrifying to be able to live according to the laws
    of foreign vocabulary
and that December might be cold and not 75 degrees so that
    he's wearing only
a t-shirt. In fact we're avoiding going home because this is
    the night when we
are going to make that provisional utopia that exists
    in the society of gestures and
the night before we were nothing but holding together tight
    beneath the sheets—and it was

enough, I'm touching you, thus was it written
    at the real beginning of the story.

6 days before the end he's at the back
of the room, he's looking everywhere else, you'd say a real bombshell
    of timidity, all
in fragments, the American and I are speaking,
    national taiwan university,
13:30 – 16:30, on "*the poetry and ideal living.*" Since
    I've got to improvise
in a foreign language I say basically whatever comes to mind, i.e.,
    that I often write
my poems in English and then translate them into French
    in order to lose dexterity, to write
directly in the occasion, in a language afflicted
    by such weakness
that it becomes simple, disabled, *I want to write the disabled*
    language of life
I say, or bizarrely, English wants to make me say,
    and certain students
listen, intrigued, and well why not, maybe it's true too,
    in any case
he rubs his hands together, you could maybe say he already
    understands that everything I say is about him,
and avoids admitting that the murmur already engulfs him,
    when later we'll
kiss beneath our dust masks inside the swarm
    of motor-scooters.
He's looking everywhere else, I smile warmly on him
    as if he were a sunflower gone
astray and strangely frightened by the light, and everyone laughs
    when it becomes obvious
that I don't know how to pronounce the *l* of difference between
    word and *world* and everyone
must have been completely confused but none of this matters
    in the end since
I managed to speak for three hours and later for the little rest
    of our days he calls me

world for fun, he says (I'm translating) *world* why, for real, do you
do poetry?
We're eating green and pink cakes that crumble
into powder
under my fingers, become the dust
adorning the light.
In fact it's very simple: it's because we must steal constantly
from absence,
and still today in the language of *wo / ni* that I'm trying to save.

The Covers

He's in his study-library because: where else? The books line the walls and spill onto the floor. Although he hates anything that separates him from the light, he's pulled the curtains to protect them. Behind, on the other side of the windows, when he goes out to walk in the streets, sits in the parks, sits outside at cafés, when he crosses the city by bike, everywhere he sees silhouettes, gaits, low-slung jeans that look like solutions. Solutions to what? If someone puts his hand against his skull for a second, say, at a particular angle and with a particular pressure he knows this means: where do you want to go, and that he will take him by force into the grand rocking of things. And that's exactly where— go figure—he wanted to go

now that I'm part
of the solicitude of everything

At the window, a movement of his hand escapes him. *Hello there* to the adolescent grass. Does he expect a sign in return? An invitation? And if so, is he capable of accepting? What would it mean to give in to the invitation of the grass? To set himself out there no matter what the weather, to drink the moisture in through his pores? To belong to an order in which all individuals are the same and henceforth it'd be the great community without difference, indifferent? Maybe. He abandons the window, turns back towards the library. The books are like a second skin for him, even a third, a fourth. The word *carapace* might be best for it. Like the tortoise: he's got the worried interrogative head of that reptile, left over from the Triassic and no longer able to recognize anything. When he pulls in his head, he too retreats into an interior where he conserves heat, stocks up calcium. It's love, said the TV series of his childhood, that's supposed to be our armor. But not for him (in fact) alone in the solitude which is in the world.

Often, he starts a type of poem he calls "etc…" Does "etc…" have one period after it, or three? someone asks him—of course not just any someone but the sort of someone half a foot away on the sofa, the sort of someone who seems authorized to declare the days open again, and now the unintimidated hours, and now the word *complicit* seems too apply to everything, there's a complicit rain falling outside, etc.

      -Only one.

      -Are you sure?

      -Yes. And so he calls them "etc...," the poems that go nowhere because time itself never stops accumulating, not in vain but without reason, and they must be continued, always and in all directions.

2 badminton players at the edge of the waves, the poc- irregular poc-poc of the green rubber ball against the wood

they're probably father & son, the kid is
skinny, his black below-the-knee shorts

already a little out of style,
he stiffens but stays 8 seconds in the ocean

unseasonably freezing, and the cicadas shrill, 17 years
underground, 2 days in the shelter of the trees, they sing

urgently to reproduce and thanks to them
us, drowned in a sort of collateral summer sizzle

and two gray war-boats

Later: he's opened the curtains so the light can rub against him. I lived alone, but I had harems of light: is that an acceptable consolation? He listens to the noises, the washing machine that makes the walls shake, especially during the spin cycle, the high school letting out, the something like a croaking of memory, like when he'd go all the way around the pond counting toads and everything seemed as simple as working himself into a landscape already on display for the sun. The trees attenuated the heat: attenuated, or made tender? Finally maybe light's our only faithful interlocutor. There are calendars to consult, and the time our dawns arrive is known centuries in advance.

Zeno was right: Achilles never managed to catch me. Even now, I keep still and Achilles doesn't catch me, isn't even visible as a point on the horizon.

Of course, he's exaggerating. Because he's still lightly beautiful, and because he gives himself easily, and because many (many) men have entered his body. It might seem like he's just seeking pleasure, but pleasure isn't important, or at least not the most important. It's simply that as soon as a man's inside him, there's a new candle at that night's window, another invincible flickering poised like a sentry at the gates. At home, he's made a map of the world and he sets a little lightbulb in it like a victor's flag at each new name lodged inside him, sheltered inside him, and sometimes he makes them blink, the scattered electric prayers of his existence.

For example, to date, Brazil: Edison, Helder, X, a student he went to pick up at his hotel whose name he's forgotten but not the gestures, he never forgets gestures. Edison's, holding his legs in a V at the edge of the bed. And Plinio who covered him in saliva and pulled violently at his breasts, Miguel who slept with him because of a *quid pro quo*, on his couch and then in his bed, Marcus who he remembers often would place his hand on his head, Marcelo the fashion designer, Vinicius the computer engineer who had the muscles of a hare, Luciano who in the middle of it said, we can stop but it was too late, he was already inside, already written into the book of guardian names.

At night, to fall asleep, he grips the foot of the night-table: it's as if, if he could be sure of not drifting, of not wandering forever, tomorrow he'll find the way out towards morning. Tomorrow he'll wake into the benevolent crackle of dawn. Tomorrow, in the lukewarm pool of light he'll be busy, he'll write one more poem—but if, as is probably the case, language exists only (by way of touching) between two bodies (at least two bodies) then what happens to literature? What happens to the solitary production of language? Could anyone write a poem that's alone and lost in the brambles, addressed to absence? Is it possible that

a sound articulated in the sprit might be identical to a gesture
performed in the world?

The child more or less age 10 perfectly child-blond
eats his messy blueberry pancake

and his brother, finally called by
his mother "Philip" (*entschuldigung* Philip

because she knocked his glass of water over
onto him) clambers up the side of the corral

to feed the goats fresh grass and to pet
the little ones and another child, lonely or just

alone, jumps on the trampoline, melancholy,
inventing in a small voice to himself a possible

inhabited universe where the essence of sadness
is fading and now the first

drops of rain

Some men more than others become places of worship for him—
but worship of existence, only. Why some and not others? He has
no idea, but it's not linked to the pleasure they might be capable
of giving. Sitting in the dirty white armchair, behind the window,
in the lotus-silence of thought, his meditations most often seek
to penetrate this lingering mystery. The latest man who has the
status of an extra church in his city: the mass of milky blond
hair on the pillow, and the morning after, when he bent his head
down over him, his sex still with the smell of last night's sperm,
he hallucinated a candle lighting itself up in the other's mouth.
For an instant, then, he's at least initiated into one of these mys-
teries: what exists is only what can be constantly caressed by him,
or embraced, or addressed by other things. Also, for example,
everything on which he breathes: the blades of grass, the ants
walking over him, the pages of the magazine he's not actually

reading, the covers of the books which are so quickly covered with dust.

Just after making love, he opens his catalog of questions since, in a certain way, he can now see fairly clearly there. They threw me some light, or into the light. Why is there no world outside of touching or why, rather, does being in the world mean being touched? Everything touched, is it saved immediately? To what degree and under what conditions can the verb *to speak* be substituted for the verb *to touch*? Is it possible to speak if the house is isolated and each room is empty? When we say, talk to yourself, like I do all the time and without stopping, in the street and in this house, is that really it? Am I at the edge of madness, if I'm speaking alone, or have I participated in the creation of another, however improbable? Let's call him my interlocutor. My interlocutor, can he be anything: a plank in the flooring, a toothbrush cup?

A book in his library: Ovid, *Metamorphoses*, written in the eighth year of our era. The stories all go one way, the same way, namely: because of their deplorable loves, humans are transformed into calm and silent objects. Thus it was for the cypress. Cyparissus was so much in love with a stag, and Phoebus-Apollo was so much in love with the boy, the stag dies, etc., and it all ends in the invention of the cypress. What would happen if the metamorphosis, for once, went the other way? If lilacs themselves changed, say (due to their scandalous behavior), into soldiers? Probably the lilacs would run everywhere, protecting us from bombs: thus do we continue to need the word "god"

to say, the samaritan lilac has come

to perfume us with his courage

He hurts you, and then immediately he heals you. It's the most perfect birth of love I could dream of. Are you still bleeding? he asks.

Another book in his library: *The Interpreter of Ardent Desires*, Ibn Arabi, around 1202. "Whenever I mention a name in this book I always allude to her, and whenever I mourn over an abode I mean her abode." And that's exactly it: love is the nostalgic elaboration of dwelling places, and still this morning—you see—we've lived it in houses full of common corridors.

Another book in his library: Peter Handke, *The Left-Handed Woman*, 1976. In it someone suffers solitude, someone's also threatened by the madness proper to solitude in its unit of habitation. (So alone is this character that she doesn't even know what to think about anymore—but is that even really possible?)

Another book in his library: *De Lumine*, Marsile Ficin, 1492 or 93. Light connects the universe: the *vinculum universi*. A reason to hope. Light passes over us while we're cleaning the windows, for example, and—provisional, passing—isn't it identical and warm, like the duration of the smallest caress? (Tranquil, peaceful light, while the cleaning seems to make things rest a little easier.)

In the park and under August the sky
announces a new storm—pools

reeds ducks, the trees vibrating
full of the color and the density of

a rainy summer, groups of friends seated in circles
talking among the scattered remains

of the picnic, chorizo chips coca-cola, or maybe
couples: guy/girl on the bank

the separating distance charged
they don't want to draw together yet and spoil

the intense cleanliness of the promise
or: one stretched out rapturously on

the other, or: arguing
at the base of the zinnias, and now he, standing,

holding her hand, talking on the phone
his mouth full of bubble gum

(strawberry), they continue to

Another book in his library: *Lectures in America*, Gertrude Stein.
Delivered in 1934 & 35. "Anybody knows how anybody calls
out the name of anybody one loves. And so that is poetry really
loving the name of anything…" And indeed we rush down the
rapids by kayak, exhausted but exalted by the volume of syllables
to produce and when, later, we come out on the final body of
water: will it be the whole world, totally whole?

Another book in his library: *De Laudibus Beatae Mariae Virginis*.
Maybe Albert the Great. Maybe around 1260. The book says
that the Virgin, after being inseminated by the word, transforms
immediately into multiple things: a wardrobe, a meadow, a foun-
tain, a bathtub, a river, the dew, the flow itself, the fortress, the
wall, the wooden chest, the flagstones, etc., really etc., infinitely.
And finally she's definition, generally: because virgin = everything
fits her, virgin = maybe I'm directly over the hive itself. And me,
each time someone inseminates me, in his way, in whatever way,
do I become the Virgin too? What does it mean, become the
Virgin? Could I become the Virgin, belong finally to the world
of limitless equality?

Another book in his library: *Contesting Tears*, Stanley Cavell,
1996. Series of stories of abandoned women. One of them says,
at the end, "Oh, Jerry, don't let's ask for the moon. We have the
stars." Conclusion: it sometimes happens that sentences turn out
to be the same thing as the hands you would have found by acci-
dent, or maybe because you drew out a map of the neighborhood
and traced, in a corner, the big red circle of YOU ARE HERE,
then you understand that's exactly the future you had hoped for:
over there on the horizon, because of a something rising (let's
call it a star), the hope that we could (again) (again? for the first
time?) live communally in the sentences.

Sometimes, he goes to the train stations to watch the arrivals and the departures because the train schedules are the closest there is to the regular catalog of mornings. (Mornings, and sunrises, and the beginnings of understanding.) At the station, usually he buys a Danish soaked with powdered sugar glaze and a large coffee, hot and watery. He sits somewhere to eat and drink, often on the marble steps, he watches people fill and empty the locks of his desire. It's a complicated system but it functions perfectly. There's always someone coming slowly towards him and leaving him slowly and leaving him ecstatic: dead inundated bee, done in by the sweet ferment of the faces. What does he come here to look for, sitting in the station, watching the people go by? Even if no one talks to him—even if nothing. Probably a conclusion like: it's impossible to inhabit a city that no one else has already inhabited.

This superiority of morning
because of its decided

and omni-desirable air, no one could wish
for his death, flies gliding into a precocious

spring, the sun generously
upon strong green affirmation & them:

he carries boxes of flowers from the truck into the shop; while smoking he sets the tables on the café terrace; he holds the mirror for the customer to decide if the glasses still look good in the day-light, why yes, since he's paid by commission; he takes off by bike

must be bound somewhere, a
helmet protecting if ever

the sacred heart of his skull, surely
some hands will soon make use of him

Solitude Weeks Autumn / Winter

1. look at the people heading for the train
it's morning, to someone
no one wants to give any money

—what? —nothing, I was just saying that the rain's
beginning to fall, the 2 small boys, brothers,
making sputtering gunfire with their mouths

can we capture the landscapes
scattered beneath every skull, deduce
the skies of 258 lives

look at the young men speaking Arabic
in the train, gather in vain
the voices, undecipherable

luckily in the book Pasternak succeeds in skimming
the duckweed from the pool of days, turn the pages
like

like running through a damp and mossy dawn
—what? —nothing   nothing   I was only saying
that the sky's not going to lift

2. the long calm open sea
from here beneath the vinèd pergolas
the sails are lines of silence

the long sea promises: when the fog disappears
duino castle shall shine
over there they have practically the same vista
a metal hood of water

but the fog's remained: selves
we're enveloped in the emotion
of an evening = with

look at the red fruits of childhood, thawing

ok the angels were nice enough
to come even if the fog, that of the old city-streets
selling *metadona heroina cocaina*

just buy a gram
for later, our vasodilation
on the colossal scale of the orgies of duino, the sea says no

3. now we're shoulder-to-shoulder, equal
it's the first sentence that came, Rockefeller Center
11pm the results are certain
around, some people
crying a long time, slowly from slavery, you
also you're just Obama-ed with joy holy
shit president-elect maybe won't change a thing
but all the seconds of your tears
on my fingers it's already
a beginning, primrose of our debt

(actually now that the plane
has cut between our hours
you receive me with such delay
I've forgotten whether
our continents are still drifting apart)

4. what I want
before his hard strong fingers and his laughs

his gray wool socks in permanent contact
with the chatter of his skin

especially the total certainty of his sitting
in the metro back on the 17th of November 2008

what I want is his skeleton, armed with love
to glide beneath me, but fragile too

and maybe he could strangle me standing in the subway

or otherwise beat up

my interior childhood
sputtering more and more strongly

like a Geiger counter
ever more worried as death touches down

and who can still hear, in the din,
the murmured directions

towards untired tomorrows & to live

5. the songs of Leonard Cohen are super useful it's true
for covering all the noises here
for burrowing back into those close winter friendships
where you live you know

with your famous blue raincoat
torn at the shoulder,
one of those apartments where we went
the elevator opened right into it I loved

you see stupidly I've equipped
the poem to seize upon the slightest shiver
when you go out and immediately the snow
coats your lashes, covers you

do you think it's possible that we breathe better,
even dead, because we talked together years ago
a nothing clanking of the words thrown out
into black dust

sometimes in fact audible
to the technologically competent

For A Few Minutes of Sunshine

For a few minutes of sunshine there was that oblique light slanting
    in the study
and everything—the couch, the pens, the laptop too—seemed
    like it was leaning
towards me with a superior tenderness. Will this suffice to make
    the scene
a bright and calm one, from now on, eternally? Almost. Ok
    it's been many days
since that effusion of consolation. Sergio and Nizar
    are the names
that went by in the interim, several times we did together
    what it takes
to be more deeply human but nothing quite the same
    as those 3 minutes
unexpected and miraculous, a slow eternity streaming
    in the light
and each instant 1 more little stone to finger against fear.
    And then yesterday
we talked online—it'd been centuries—I was reminded
    of the glorious days
of long ago when the rain condensed itself in delicate little balls
    of dragonfly
in the middle of the super-humid air & our hours by motorbike
    & the flea market
under the highway bridges where I bought for the equivalent of
    two euros
a green army jacket with your country's slogan written on the back:
    fraternity devotion
sincerity. I love you. But then immediately it must be clarified:
    what I? what you?
and the verb *to love*, is it really the type of word,
    omnipotent,
that brings something about simply by being spoken, cf. Austin?
    i.e. does *I*
love you mean that the shower where I sucked you off each morning
    is now preserved forever in a warm eternity?
Who knows, perhaps. And yet I continue loving you
    indefatigably,

even now that we're living on opposite ends of the earth,
    and it doesn't seem
to matter. You see, it's here and I'm looking for a dialect for you
    & for us, to shelter
the tireless things. Again, many days. I watch over the remaining
    light as it
drains away and I speak on guard against the death
    that comes:
the yellow jonquils are going to fade, soon everything will be hard
    and crumbling, like the inside of
stale bread. I speak. The conversation is of course with
    absolute silence.
It's a solo contraction inside my room. And
    then yesterday I met
another you to add to your face. When I asked him,
    dance please
I want to watch you, because he's a dancer / writer /
    cashier, mostly
unfortunately for him a cashier, and he moved his hands
    like tears.
It was as moving as the radical sadness let's say of throwing up
    at night
& you're alone & there isn't anyone. One of our next plans
    is to kiss
at the top of the Eiffel Tower one more thing
    I've never done
and my god it's probably stupid but it happens
    so rarely
that our lives are on the right sides of our skins. Up
    there I could
confess to you the ideas I have for each one of you. You know,
    how to liberate your faces
with a sort of general visa is the question that preoccupies me.
    The sad part comes
later when he, too, will have gone back to living in another place
    on Googlemaps
and if you type Medellin, Girardota he's there, breathing,
    prisoner of that grid

of streets completely lost at the muddy foot of the mountains.
      Even if lost surely
isn't the right word, just given the number of people
      who live there. I think I
only wanted to say you, too, added to the removal of obsolete
      solutions.
There was no reason to think the Ancients were wrong
      to explain:
winter overwhelms us and at each new moon an adjective
      must be
added, like: stripped bared left behind. Well ok.
      Anyway. Many
days etc. Unequipped. It's the 23rd of April and I guess
      I'm still living
even if the source of that soothing light is now
      quite exhausted. Önder
is one name that slipped through in the interval. What more to
      put down in the booklet
of rememberences? That the Bosphorus out the hotel window
      looks like
it still has to get through something, probably us. That we've
      descended the street, through construction
all the way to the Galata Bridge, farther, despite
      his injured knee,
that we ate fried fish on the bridge badly protected
      from the cold wind,
it's called the Golden Horn but names are always deceiving, or at
      least more deceiving
than, for example, the body. In the course of the following nights
      that found us
huddled together I wondered if he too would become
      anonymous in the spaces
between the words I and love and you. I.e. does I love you mean
      you ejaculated
inside me a maximum number of times in a
      minimum number of days?
Yes, well, as well. That's my new definition for it. Incredible,
      in fact, that someone on the phone

just told me when I was explaining to her that my whole life
    consisted
of building an overpopulated *you* to help me glide from day to day
    all the way to the end
peacefully the death: it's like Faulkner, for whom fornication
    was the only thing
that made the blood survive. So then I looked
    on the internet
and I came up with this phrase, useful
    for everything: "you have committed
fornication: but that was in another country, and besides, the
    wench is dead,"
(T.S. Eliot, more or less). Is the phrase I love you maybe
    the road
to finally the other country where life resembles the light
    when light is the subject of the verb
to push through, resembles an empty intersection, resembles the
    arrival of the last look?
It's the next morning and still you want to share me except
    I have to swear first
that the Armenian genocide was a myth and I give in.
    You see I only have one single
principle, to do what makes a life unfold. I swear it and we come.

The Loves That Stay

I

If Yi Jui was the case
and Julio is still perhaps the case and it
will never again be the case that Bogdan despite a deep desire
to the contrary and thus if p
is true when B. (for example) puts his hand on me
with his proud smile for now being able to dictate
the events happening thus
it's 99% certain that not-p if
that type of certainty exists   let's say it's impossible
and the world makes itself scarce but we can
within 1% or so calculate the sadness beneath the CD
    & empty January
on the return train
towards nothing and
finally a subtle outline waiting on the quay

II

    ...and at the pool today
grand opening of the summer   the sun
sympathizer to infantine splashes

    I forgot to put in my contacts and I lose

        ...that blurry promise 1m85
of very calm forecast
as if I were going swimming in the deep tranquil basin
where each lap makes each promised tomorrow last a little longer

III

At the birthday party
mentally accompanied by yesterday's videostore salesman
who wrapped the gift…
        then dancing endlessly
will that be enough to make a special sonnet
where all the order
gathered yesterday into the combed perfection
of his hair

…all the messedup order might sweetly
spread

IV

In the crowded night   following
engine damage and we apologize for the   finally
      the suburban station
calm and the street running along the aqueduct   not so
long before the rain…
there are also 2 shapes
on which desire settles, like over the possible trees
of healing and everything
confirms the existence
of nights and selves   it's the same
surprise as thousands of times before   why
are faces
and arms beneath t-shirts simply enough
                  …who knows
if we'll be held close in the occasional posthumous rush of things

V

definitely he took a nap

...another session at the pool
in the shower with too much soap face to face and especially at
    the exit
your hoodie says Russia   and how
so that you might stay
forever and at the end light up again in   candle of leanness
unfaithful to fragility
and that I'll use if necessary   who waits supremely for the bus
to soothe the agony

VI

For days already I've been in mourning
for   ....the time of our
existence   he waited for hours
and I arrived drenched in sweat
from having biked so fast   we very thoroughly make
love in the room where the workers
next door are replacing the windows and the next day
he goes back to Santiago
in Chile   did I give him signs, gestures enough
for him with his 21 fewer years
to   to vaporize myself in time
when   it's later &
his own list where   September afternoon
dislocated   a tongue drooling over his feet

VII

Voices & laughter of virile Spanish youth
tossed into the water in the pool
        on the other side of the cliff   I suppose in order to
withstand
the heavy-duty heat   and immediately 1 more whole volume
of exile after a number of them
already verging on infinity   it's always on the other
side of course of no matter what boundary
where one could
gather up the breaths   I stay
in the hotel room no air-conditioning the time
that the silence might bring back and cancel out
                                and in the street along the beach
no longer a single neck willing
to let itself be touched & together to enjoy the little decks for two
        beside the sea

VIII

we only have a dampened calendar & in it we're erased

IX

In a scholarly article Benveniste writes
      you are the *allocuté* of the instant
which means, I'll explain it, he
who deploys the predicates of the inexhaustible present   i.e.
if I say *you* then any other verb then everything becomes
that which is done by you
more or less quickly   of action...
I'd love to believe...
but there's a frieze in gold and blue on the art-nouveau building
on the other side of the street
and when I lower my gaze
behind the traffic mostly gray and black busses & cars
down towards the sidewalk and towards nothing
where you should magically have appeared
if language worked for real

X

   ...   winter's winning
degree by degree even if the sky
resists with lovely ultimate blue   the faces
wrenched from the passing bicycles, pressed
against the stomach like the warm
sauna towels   it's the best
definition of the poem all
the science developed so that language might follow
your track

XI

Someone's waiting at the station just
beside the posters that announce the strike…

XII

       shoulders relaxed like across
the finish line later and it's   a sort of miracle
full of the pagan sun
see language descend
into the world and   we speak
mouths directly in the midst of things
as if   I say it while breathing out....
the train to the airport was direct and for once it worked
     the plane
was simply there

XIII

it's evident, it's starting
his skin the   in the wake
          the worker

XIV

and to live
it has to   be in the end a story
the same one we've been telling ourselves
forever   in the metro someone raises
his head
flowing hair   beneath a gray hat
lovesick cliché and the crutch supports it

                    ....winter leaving his mouth the metro
runs along i.e. people get on and get off
we're together enough

STÉPHANE BOUQUET is the author of several collections of poems and—most recently—a book of essays on poems, *La Cité de paroles* (2018). He has published books on filmmakers such as Sergei Eisenstein and Gus Van Sant, as well as screenplays for feature films, non-fiction films, and short films, and has translated poets including Paul Blackburn, James Schuyler, and Peter Gizzi into French.

LINDSAY TURNER is the author of *Songs & Ballads* (2018). Her translations from the French include *adagio ma non troppo*, by Ryoko Sekiguchi (2018) as well as a book of philosophy by Frederic Neyrat, *Atopias* (co-translated with Walt Hunter, 2017). She is the recipient of a 2017 French Voices Grant for her translation of Stéphane Bouquet's *Vie Commune*.

NIGHTBOAT BOOKS

Nightboat Books, a nonprofit organization, seeks to develop
audiences for writers whose work resists convention and transcends
boundaries. We publish books rich with poignancy, intelligence,
and risk. Please visit nightboat.org to learn about our titles and
how you can support our future publications.

The following individuals have supported the publication of this
book. We thank them for their generosity and commitment to
the mission of Nightboat Books:

Kazim Ali
Anonymous
Jean C. Ballantyne
Photios Giovanis
Amanda Greenberger
Elizabeth Motika
Benjamin Taylor
Peter Waldor
Jerrie Whitfield & Richard Motika